Under dark under branches

ISBN 978-1-928476-50-4
ebook ISBN 978-1-928476-51-1

Deep South, Makhanda
contact@deepsouth.co.za
www.deepsouth.co.za

Distributed in South Africa by
Blue Weaver Marketing and Distribution
https://blueweaver.co.za

Distributed worldwide by
African Books Collective
PO Box 721, Oxford, OX1 9EN, UK
https://www.africanbookscollective.com/publishers/deep-south

Cover painting: Mindy Stanford
Cover design: JMS Design
Text design and layout: Liz Gowans

Under dark under branches

Joan Metelerkamp

deep south

1

The photograph on the lid
of our sixties' Christmas biscuit tin
stick stuck on the falling
water there where we sometimes stopped
at the side of the road   on the way to fetch the boys –
your hand held at the edge of the edge –
our reality   our river
over the rocks
in the middle of the water-
fall falling the stick stuck forever
and ever our water-fall our river –
Mother

*

I am four –
looking up at the black of the leaves
against the sun   running like water
over his pram   is it I   or he   my baby brother
who is seeing –

even then   look up at the plane   I am four
                    does he see this light   this shadow
under branches   under leaves   free
                    wheeling patterns against the light –

blind wonder of light patterns of black

     *

Through plantations across the river
can feet recall   can smell
                  sight   remember
or is it only the black and white photograph
burnt now   gone   burnt into the inner retina

remembered   dappled-skinned chidren
fixing in the way of memory
an after-image   like the bruise of love –

close second brother and I
running through the pines without any clothes
over resinous needles and cones
wolf children we knew
our mother's myths and legends
sharp-faced   azure-eyed   wolves
we knew were continents   ages away –
free feral kids   filtered through shadows of tall trunks
hot breath   resin   the fall of drumming feet
calling out to each other
like birds   wild children free of any words
swishing swashbuckling sticks –
at last the cleft   fringe of bush   where the stream
cleared its cleave over the stones and into its cool
falling   streaming to its own clear cool

                  *

Boys running –

                barefoot along the gravel up to the dairy
did I think I was one of them   the boys –

what I learned as a pre-school girl
as I lay in the hay above the cows
lifting their tails to the sweet smell of flopping
pissing   hissing
while the boys whispered   giggling like girls   *they're girls*
the hard-full dung-stained velvet-soft teats   I learned
something I didn't have or had what
no boy would ever want   all that   my father kept up
the game of *thanks my boy!*

                Ashton Tarr the vet testing
the herd did he think I was one of the boys
holding the dish with the syringe
didn't he know they were gone to school
                to Miss Stacey's –

running through the dust to the mud hut
you pass on the corner
the bare-foot kids   like you   running
and not like you   running where you're not allowed
  over the grid
on the curve of the dirt road
while you rattle past next year with your brothers
and Lahksman in the cab   the milk truck's ten-gallon cans
rattling on the back on the way to your separate mud hut
in the garden of the housemaster's house
amongst flaming maples and maternal planes

lined up along the edge of the field
of the white-boys-only brick-only boarding school
but in your hut five kids in each class in a row on their bench
scratching the blackboard top of the bench-desk-top
chalk   slates   smoke (Miss Stacey's and the winter fire's)
learning with each   letter   in the   lines   on the   slate
the plain pleasure   of writing   for writing's sake

Claire with the brass bell running in clanging
tea-time tea-time and time
for Red Rover red-faced on the grass and time
to face yourself the tin hut the pit
beneath the wooden plank and its hole
where you are on your own alone with the loose leaved
scratching Jeyes-paper like tracing paper

but back inside your brothers are with you
in class two and standard one rows
with the big boys   behind you

and one day Janet and John   jump
over the page and Rover catches his ball and
in the end you choose *Shopping with Mother*
for your prize –

Christmas-time summer-time sea-watermelon-time
Christmas-beetle-like-tinnitus-time
frog snake bare-foot dam-time
river stones and biscuit tin and cake time

and Jesus! how could you forget supper-time
and no-screaming-in-the-bath with the boys
the whole rigmarole of drinks   end-of-the-line
even in holiday-time
even for the boys
Grownups Time

*

Cold sweat and lurch
up and out of bed
to run down the passage to tell your mother who will know
you know
something to do with *groot-Ouma*
whom you call Ouma although she is Oupa's mother
she's not here anymore   not there
Ouma

         there is something
         flapping under the stone of your chest
         in the branches of your breathing
         like black birds pecking and you know
         you are sweating

but
morning
                  and out past *thank you for your courtesy*
sign swinging on the pole at the grid
as you go out
and back again past the waterfall
and back up the dirt road back to the grid back
into the farm
please drive slowly   children and cattle crossing

in the afternoon wind   cacophony of soapbox wheels
across the gravel
back up to the border of the grid
forbidden road you and your brother venture out into –
         shock in the lop-sided tied-on rearview mirror

over the bombastic car bonnet   smiling wife of *Imali-liyavusa*
so close you can see her teeth

*

The deep pull away
                    from Maritzburg's valley
lit like Granny's necklace –
lights and voices and the dark and the stink –
and our mother crying   waving to the boys
and our father on the platform –

nothing of the time in Pretoria can I remember –
bits of it she told me much later –
her friend   the stillbirth   a boy
or was it that stranger
                    misnomer   miscarriage –

so Toekie came back with us –
second daughter with the pale face and the long dark hair –
through the tunnels of the valley of a thousand hills
through the cuttings
we stood in the swaying passage:
ecstasy of slow advance   krantz appearing with wild
strelizia   thicket   bush dense and
disappearing again   under the weight
of the earth   under the earth
to feel   to suppose
after the first terror   it would be alright   we would come out

all gone forever –
Toekie   the first
(her youngest   Blonkie   as young as she and I on that
ancient train)
Biffy   her mother   who would never recover

Bimbi   her friend   my mother   forever travelling that way
to take herself away   out of the way
                              way out of reach

        *

Just a small farm girl with the corner of grubby cross-stitch
balled in a fist on the foot of the steps to the senior's hall

white girls only boarding school   *houses*   no more or
was it   is it   no less real than Brownies' fairy groups –

named for crooked patriarchs *Buxton Athlone Somerset Rhodes*
classrooms glaring white in the sun   big yellow

country-wide history book and poor Miss Kneale
what did she care about colonial officials' acute corruption –

white on our church gloves   Sunday dresses white
blue our blazers   by the time we were seniors

crazy suspenders for stockings like a belt
for a *sanitary towel* worn under regulation *flour bags*

don't wear tights   stockings   *gocking-shoes*   gloves   hats
under the stifling Maritzburg sun   but before that

Brownies' groups   like school houses' fantasies   certainties
lace-ups   ties and toggles   and Judy is there

with her Breck-blonde dead-straight hair   clean and shiny
as the lacquered lid of the brand-new piano

like her mother's Breck advert Grace-of-Monaco
photo lying on top of the piano –

but not Judy's brother who hung on the door frame
to breathe   the whispered cataclysm of *asthma*

unreal   real as   *eternity*   breathlessness's
cold-sweat sibilant-twin *non-existence*

*

Meanwhile demonic possessions of
tokoloshe and *mafufunyane* go on at home

under beds on bricks   in the heat of tomato picking
down at the river   women fainting in the fields

mealie-fritters burning like rot-gut curry for supper
in the holidays and is it revenge (four praying mantises

like the four horsemen of the apocalypse
dive-bombing the supper table and even in my shame

I run like a girl)   summer night dead-dark and alive
eight already and the drums drumming deep into the night –

revenge like my precious disappeared
turquoise bathing-costume with its useless

white and blue striped belt and brass buckle
cut up in filthy strips dug up from its burial –

and who was responsible   she who was so dark
and soft our father thought so too   our mother

then   in the little play at the fete
the W.I.   and she's painting her nails

on the stage as she doesn't answer the phone –
I see as clearly as seeing that day for the first time

pink and white ice-cream shaped into a cake
what they think of her   everyone is laughing

and it is the telephonist of the party line
they are laughing at   and my mother

they are laughing with   like they say to me
my mother and father   we're laughing *with* you

so why am I not laughing   *hello   exchange?*
double one three oh! three shorts no longs

but the one when someone wants the exchange –
she is painting her nails and sometimes breathing

hard down the line that goes nowhere but
into their weird hilarity   complacency   camaraderie

confusing as when it's my turn on the make-shift stage
with the others in the John Orr's parade

turquoise costume followed by indigo taffeta whispering
radical black spider on the sleeve   web across the skirt

     *

Hearing again the long gone andante

the forgotten sonata played in the sweaty YMCA
in Maritzburg   down in the dip
close to that sluggish river   the Dusi   the long
                    long ago piano exam –

let it repeat   recapitulate
da capo return this time reiterate
its tender refrain
as if it were simple and here again   resonating
repetitive opening phrases
playing more lightly   less earnestly   daily

forget the old authorities   the old injunctions
like old old lines learnt by heart
the play under the trees in the school quad
I a young Greek girl running
from the men through the trees –
bare-foot Iphigenia over the needles and stones –

by heart   by heart
had I the tongue of Orpheus I'd use my magic now

sixteen   stood in front of the school   said Jesus said
of those to whom much is given   much will be required

as if we even knew what we'd been given
how much and how much of what we needed

what was required   what was always required   what others
required   wake

from that nightmare
of history
split duplicitous black and white history   dead
body of history
and the raucous crows who pick at it –

*

There   that page is torn out
old stories   done
gone into   nothing
but memory   and cousin-at-one-remove remembered
hearsay

burnt all the old photographs
letters   piles in cardboard files
carbon copies shored up with all the old originals
little hand written letters   folios of type
in the old *jongmanskas* that stood on the stoep
also ash   done now   gone in the fire that took them all out –

old images still old thoughts like lack of faith
repeat themselves still
firing neurons along the old habitual pathways
like under the diaphragm burning the solar plexus –
little ways of thinking little ways of holding –
can't douse the old thoughts again and again
can't stand aside
get out of my own way   recover –

placed the desk under the window
here   in this still new-to-me country
under the pussy willow's shelter the hawthorn's
little-leafed indifference

old stories like old habits like old skin
peeled away peeling along the old cracks
revealing the tender place

ways of holding still from that other place –

little footsteps little bare feet over the grass
stopped for a moment   waiting
and running then running down the hard dirt road
soft feet from another time and another place
freely through the reeds
across the clay   the little weir at the wall at the dam
the *Amanzimnyama*   the black water
running to get away from the sign
the sign in the long grass   they said   said
trespassers   as I understood   would be executed –

south west   this summer of this north comes
with the cool clarity of a childhood autumn
under the hills   *Endebeni*   quiet and clarity
of a Sunday   sick   all the rest
gone off to the river and only you and your mother

old ways old ideas old habits old roads like the road
from *Endebeni* followed sixty two sixty three years ago
five long miles along the dirt
the twists and the ruts and the dust to Lidgetton
standing in the back of the old Morris Minor –
"Phoebe Morris" smelling of damp and old leather –

and on on the tar on to Howick past
the ones you could name
and the ones you can't –

forgotten   lost in the shadows
there the daughter who could never get up
only whispered amongst you
(a pale curtained room   a black metal bed
someone's sister who could not move nor speak) –

the fire came and took them all   all the stories
typed   in their reams all the letters albums and archives
mother carefully collected collated
for the fire to take them all
like her own mother   her husband's family letters
before she snuffed her own life out –

pick up the thread like those legendary ones
your mother first told you of
Ariadne (Theseus who forgot to put up his sails) Penelope
(done all that nocturnal picking apart   repetitive doubt
 knotted knitting in the cupboard   done with it)

wait   forget all the old thoughts that wake you at night
shouting
in your sleep wide awake now give them leave to go
listen   rain   rain beginning again beginning
to rain again rain
quiet   like rained-on horses in the rain
under muddy blankets
in the field in front of you
wait

*

2

Out of intimate caring came
the one-eyed nurse
                   turning the father's diminishment –

she who spooned tenderly   shredded beef   mashed squash
knowing how he hated it –
or was it only his daughter who hated
what his partner believed
what the eye
              doesn't see the heart
                              doesn't grieve after –
turning the small of his back for the daughter to see
the shriveled skin
like the top of rice pudding   pulled back –

like out of another age the mother
to the brothers in the bath
pull your foreskins back   remember –

as after the father left his withered patrimony
the sad celtis   white stinkwood   and the house
to the wasps in the ceiling corner
                   the brothers as if after burning
shedding another skin –

                   exposed the spreading sore

        *

Under the weight of the dead   we were born   into
the light-shade of the plane   under the wings of its leaves
the scent of farm dung after rain   we came
to soften their will   their dogged passion   their need
to get free of the dead and the just-dead
done and undone   the un-love of suicide and war
(to give up at last on her bed with the very same gun)

now   here   now at night they come
the dead and the half-dead and the far from me
saying they won't pay my husband their debt
as it was   really   in his job in the municipality
they mock me egregiously   but I see what I need
 a tender friend   like our far-gone G.P.   at home   to ask me
the question itself *what ails thee* giving the mythical remedy

*

Underneath the desk
a large book like a footstool   a handmaiden
underneath the soles of feet
soles of shoes   under the soles of shoes a book
brought by the handmaidens

heavy is the sound   a large book   heavy
is its weight   the weight of over-ripe fruit
weighing down a branch   or the bear in hibernation
who sits on your chest while you look backwards –

wake up   please wake up   almighty God
what shall I do   wake up as I used to

*

It appears   when you least expect
bare-foot up from summer-silent rest

stand still   wait   step back as if everything were
real and you weren't imagining anything

everything to be expected   face it
move away   if it doesn't move at all if it refuses

to shift   wait   if you can't get back to the door
wait for as long as it takes   wait for a frog

looking for shade   wanting the internal cool
where is your father   even then where is he

why can't he lift you out of the way
shut that door firmly

if you are looking out as you were
when you were seven riding across the bridge

and on the other side the willow like Medusa's hair
alive   can it be what you think you hardly dare

look into the branches   writhing —
as in that stone-staring face you've faced

obliquely   you've made yourself glance at   slantly
quickly turning the page in *Finding Out* —

heart like "Pegasus' wings   beating together"
comfort your mare   murmur into her mane

it's all alright   they won't harm you   they're little
let them be   let them wait –

it waits   still
coiled on the carpet under the desk

        *

Boomslang   puffadder   cape cobra
nightadder in the dark you stood on
in the veggie garden
holding hard to your mother's hand –
one who came to your recurring nightmare
where you were lying suffocating   dying
under the hedge near the dairy –

old neural pathways   you keep going down
the dorsal-vagal ancient reptile
branch of that nerve keeping you
half-human   mock-dead
when you aren't shouting yourself awake in the night
the dead waking you to shout loud enough
to wake the dead   only it's only you
and your husband next to you who wake –

look up   look out on this northern island
where you are now –
little gentle pussy-willow in the window –
seasons upside down yes
but soft cadences of easy voices
in the ancient lanes in any weather here

        *

The view of the valley
the slow snaking river   the sea

where we built our house   the light
in the rafters turning the roof

upside down into
the hull of a coracle   an ark

once my mother had rowed herself
out   all night

down that river of night out
out to the mouth   to the sea –

all of this holding
nothing   fragrant as air

tarconanthus   watsonias   ericas
wild olive at the place of the reservoir —

fire-fighting-water-useless-reservoir —
all that   burning to the bone

to the raw back of the dune
dreaded   then known

deadly paradox of fire

         *

35

Newlands   a new way   the old woman
with the warm hands and the welcoming voice
teacher who opened her door   on the threshold
of your own third age
showing you how to stop
doing the old stuff   hearing the old injunctions
as you looked up at the planes
Cape Town   *mother city*   you had driven and driven
this way   it comes to you   what it is is it is always
the mountain in its female folds   its ancient forested flanks
behind the brilliant cyclorama sky the real mother of all
loveliness   aloneness   all in this moment it is
showing you and you're seeing now and now and now

*

Listen   I am here now   what did I think –
I could belong anywhere

I'm walking this side in this country   learning how to think
sensing the stones through sensible shoes
ankles loose   knees forward and away
gravity   my friend   helping my spine lightly
head tipping slightly
on top of the atlas –
brain at the back of the skull taking light in letting
light in –

single stalks and ears   just here
bending where the hill rolls back
and up into wave of bleached gold
as in *resilience*   as in our family crest
three wheat ears and carved below them
flecti non frangi   bent not broken

wheat loosely alive in the sudden sun –
but the close stalks quite still and the hill
a wave   in this sudden clarity   clarity itself
to approach indirectly as in surfing the wave
sun on the face of each clear   flexible ear

*

The tender notes of passing
I thought were played for mothers
sorrow's tender syncopations

like sussurating leaves shaking
these feelers of maternal branches tentatively
tracing syncopations of the sun on the shiny

side of the pussy-willow
lit from beneath
so where does the shadow

come in   tenderness tending to wildness
the wind   now   and here here and now
converge in chiaroscuro bruise of adagio

and on   like steps   on
through threnody for the place that is gone
the people   gone

the creatures like the two mongooses
alert at the edge of the fynbos
like the curious dead come back to see

the sea the wind the river
the dune with its slow reptilian slope
growing back at the burn the ridge on its back

after the fire begin again like the poet mourning
her sister who turned savagely one summer
to sight read right through the deaf master's sonatas

*

What was I imagining
driving up Louis Botha avenue   1980
the thought as if from nowhere
the thought police hear what you are thinking –

the opening of the state theatre
the director of the opera   director of the whole charade
hissed to his wardrobe mistress
who brought me this   it's only five foot two –
impossible platform shoes to compensate
like the punishing patent leather inches-high heels
on the stones of the school at Thabazimbi
where we brought them a play to play for them
black hill of iron   heat of steel
hier kom die moffies en hoertjies van TRUK
all those little sausage rolls and *melkterts* for nothing
curling up at the edges with disgust of the staff-room

all all of that left like long ago
uniformed patrolled Pretoria itself   and the country too
like love split in two   let go

we are hungry   in the name of Jesus
we are crying on you

                 *

Undo it all   take it all off   this self-protection
like long ago uniforms
in Pretoria in the 80s – schoolkids bank-tellers teachers
policemen domestic workers rubbish-collectors   even actors –

              wanting nothing   but that old worn down
sand feel of sand on skin down at the wild-side
flat on my back lengthening and widening
on sand and salt water cool
undulating under the rock in the pool in the rock –

not even sun-screen   nothing   skin to the sun
nothing to do   undoing what's unnecessary   done
the months and months the years of muscular locks

sand like skin shining in darker
arms   feet   sand like underbelly   released

              *

Put my ear to a shell not expecting anything
it's just an exercise you say but I expect
more really   urgency   necessity   sound
of the real sea   put my ear to the air
minus two degrees   trees   ashes here
not even sighing not even shaking   utter nothing I can hear

sound of the southern-cross sky far
ululating fiery-throated nightjar
frogs   crickets   lone lowing of the mothers
in the valley
bull calves already taken to the pens

long-gone laugh of my mother
in my father's story Tom Lowe laughing with my father
all the way down to the butcher   you can hear her

      *

Like a bull-frog outside the bathroom window there at home
the woodpecker call here now
knocking
let it in
let in the rattling bull-frog dinky-tractor-call
then the knocking knocking   reminding
you again down this avenue of ashes this hurrying
stream saying
you can breathe as if you were allowing
yourself
to be breathed
no-one with a gun or a knife   no-one begging
at your gate   *in the name of Jesus   crying on you*
you can forget it you can turn your back
to the sun to let it through you can forget
you can remember *my country*
is the whole world you can begin again
to allow your ankles hips neck
to be a little freer

*

He is at the bedroom window-sill
holding out his hand in abeyance –
tea-strainer hovering like a butterfly
or a butterfly net   as if he were hoping
for the season to swell   to catch
more than the thought he is following

everything hovers for a moment –
he's pouring the tea   encouraging me
to get up and out of my
comfort zone under the duvet

only the two of us
now we are Oupa and Ouma
                    and the old feather bed

time to begin he's saying again
though he doesn't quite say it
he's pouring the tea thinking aloud
put action first without over-thinking

but I'm lying back thinking   listen   I'm doing something else
learning what *not* to do to let butterfly psyche be
unhinging her wings gently   landing softly –

woken again to the impossible width
of the quiet the whole place still
under house arrest
trees   fields   silent still
present   continuous   continuing

(nights the wave after wave of waking   shouting
at the edge
of the bed
            lurching into sitting
and back inside the dark of the wave
dumping me and
dumping me   dragging me
across the stones   and into the shallows)

            *

Turn back   inside   drag myself back
in to this smell of damp
to the internal smell faintly like a long-ago aunt's house –
not the smell of un-love I used to think it was
something un-lived   un-realised
more stale   more mouldy and animal –

remember!   she was once Anna-Belle!
when they were all still dark-haired and in love
my father   her brother   my laughing mother
Anna
bell!   they would call her

long before she turned

                                    to singing deliberately
don't worry   be happy

                        at the same time as she turned
to Jesus and more
and more wine

I was the only girl   with her
not *only a girl*   with Ann
in her overblown turquoise plumage
like the wings of the little common or garden
                                    brown-hooded kingfisher
who used to keep watch on the pole on our stoep

plump-breasted   plump-bellied pipping

giggling on the couch tipping the wine glass   tippling –

sometimes I see her
sad faced   and florid   fixing her smile
back at me in this bathroom mirror –
hooded eyes like my father's
chubby cheeks like a kingfisher's
and mine when I was four
and lay with her in the bath
wondering why her breasts were
not round mounds like my mother's –

and then which is then which was now
I am standing
behind the front seats while my father drives
my baby brother wrapped in the shawl
on our mother's lap and I ask
is he blind like a kitten or a puppy
and when does he open his eyes

and when you ask but does a brown-hooded kingfisher
even have chubby cheeks I answer like a child
I don't care   I don't care   that's how she is to me
now that she has been given me as a kingfisher my aunt
in the turquoise she used to love
in my mother's garden –
beloved irises' purple plumage
abandoned against the bedroom where she lay on the bed
with the gun —

like the kingfisher who used to visit me
alone   at the top of the hill   at home   when the children

had left like martins
from the crumbling clay under the eaves

all of them gone   the garden the garden the garden
home   farm   country
children   fathers and mothers   aunts uncles and cousins
kingfishers
boubous   sombre bulbuls   house martins
into nightmare from out of nowhere again –

in this morning's reprieve
before I turn inwards
in this English country garden
is there anyone
in the sticks of thick hedge here   calling me

*

I wanted to make it something as if I were making
my way a journey to love like making love not only like
Asphodel that greeny flower in *Journey to Love*
like a road-trip
the long meanderings like dirt tracks going there and back
to the Cape from a trip to the lowveld
via Clocolan as we used to joke a story that gets somewhere
eventually
everyone bored and asking you to get there get on with it
missing the dip through the dip windows wide
dust and sun time for a moment
            taking you freely there –
I told the ones I found myself virtually among I told them
about Clocolan in the *Free State*
            and the sadness the freight of that *free* –

zooming in in detail in this writing group
wanting to help me
they tell me to take small steps –
four lines only four words for the journey
like Sydney's *with how sad steps* –
what I haven't told them
what I miss most about home the moon and its rising
over the dune over the valley liquid gold in the river –

I told them of the two hundred million year old
hills that lie like two hundred million year old
ancient lizards likkewaans as you come back
from the lowveld via Clocolan through the eastern
Free State the Karoo

I thought I'm not only thinking about some ancient creature
    mock-dead   half-alive
more like the paradox of where I've just been what's taken
    with me
on the journey home
cold-blooded crocodiles
allowing themselves   to sun themselves
on the dry bed
of the Luvuvu
like my own arms resting on my stomach   supine

leave the long way round for your novel   they quip
how can I make the connection   the confluence   clearer
can they understand how close the confluence
how close those crocodiles lie
to the warm naked legs
of the fishermen   of the Limpopo –

in the end   I finally get it   give them what they want

Arrival
Terminal
Baggage
Bus out

*

3

It's scored in black and white
like photos from my childhood burnt now
with the homestead not even ash any more not even
anything –

a military field hospital   lines of tents   the siege of Mafeking
in the war where   grandmother Joan
your father died on one side   and you were only two
your future husband on his own split family's side
split between the two sides   no side
evacuated out of Pretoria –
Oupa George down at the sea
where Fuschang ate his *swimming trunks*
poor cow   licking the salt off the line –

and you   grandmother
where your mother nursed and your father died
in the siege of Mafeking   as I was told as a child
but what did it mean   cholera   unappeasable hunger –
and you   learning to talk and to run among the wounded
the sick the stink of the tents the leather the horses
the guns   heat   flies
the stench of the veld and the sun –

old photograph   two lines of tents
and in the forefont outside the flaps   the men in stretchers
and stretching behind them the sun and the veld
and somewhere in the background
your mother in buxom uniform
with the white veil and the cross

and the long grey skirt in the heat
and somewhere your father already just buried   Mafeking
military hospital where you learnt to walk and to run
among the tents and the heat and the sun
and the stench of dying men

and so long ago now   am I just making this all up
playing with little scraps of story
sticks and stones little broken bones little blessed horses

daughter and daughter and daughter –
I failed your daughter as she failed you

always I will have failed your daughter my mother
failed to hear the plea
underneath the plea
when she asked me
would I help her to die would I even listen could not
hear what I hear now   now
I am closer I hear her
will you help me will you not fail me
as all the men fail me –

left her to herself   as she left you to
take the gun to
unlove of un-love

*

Oupa George   and if I turn softly
suicide-grandmother unknown-Joan
                              and if I turn
obliquely I hear them come softly through the lockdown
here next to the sound
of the washing machine spinning

here   like the little old woman come in her brown
in the corner of Oupa's sitting room   waiting
for his return –
his four-in-the-morning morning swim –

pungence of pawpaw for breakfast   law books in rows
strange African masks in his Alexis Preller paintings his
room hung with strange clarity of morning sun
as he told me where she'd been
sitting in the corner   waiting –

Oupa with his deeply ridged fingernails
white shirt and tie over his *boep*
what pain has he come to help me through
what sickness – like the sickness a hundred years gone

in the pandemic of flu
at home in Pretoria
he helped the doctor
whose name I've forgotten all the people
whose names I never knew
he tended and nursed and helped
and couldn't help

they came to him   stood in his sitting room –
the dead   literally   beyond
the couch where he'd slumped
after his night-shift   dawn –

he knew their presence   presenting themselves
they came to him
to comfort his exhaustion   thank him –

what did it mean that kind of prescience   vision

what did I think   did I think leaving
                    the country   my country   the sea
        the house and the farm to the fire
and my brother's house and his farm to the fire
that took all the letters all the pictures all the old
photographs
all the old ancestors the dead
                    could take them from me

        *

Old man   atheist acutely conscious
          of his own intelligence
sat at his desk making notes
from an ancient Greek version of the bible
just before the end –

his deeply ridged fingernails
his arm around my torso my head to his *boep*
his breath smelling of angostura bitters
house sweet with paw-paw and dust of books –

Oupa George – the first book I wrote –
careful cursive of the dipping pen
between the ready ruled lines

dutifully beginning at the beginning —
Hudson   his father   riding his bike like hell
along the dusty streets of Pretoria
to call the doctor –

as if suddenly sick of it all   to end
the chronicle   *his wife*   I write   the mother of all
euphemisms   *died* –
how long did it take
for her to come out of the dark out of old letters
for me to see clearly through the stories
the scrap of the lamp shade marked with an x
at the bullet's tear
where she turned the gun to the temple –

I open his uncle's *Versamelde Werke*
Dear Joanie –
this is still the best stuff
in Afrikaans – anyhow in poetry –
from Oupa George.
2 July 1970

post boer-war highveld *Winter Nag*
on the cover   Eugene's insect-like script
rhyming *genade* with *skade*
black ink's meticulous
little lettering linking

blessing   destruction
damage and mercy and grace

   *

4

It could be you and your daughter
in the start of this autumn last of summer sun
              it could be
you and your mother in the warmth of the last late
sun through the sitting room window and she could be
stitching the pattern of the little birds and the strawberries
emerging from their speckle-patterned wool

outside the sorrowing celtis receives
all the thoughts with open
late summer branching and the leaves are just beginning
to turn and you or your daughter or your mother
turn
to look out of the sitting room window
              the weight of the sun
falling
across you

          *

We are talking about pattern
                    and reading pattern
and who is talking   we sad poet-strangers come together
over the little screen over
                    what matters   what means
to what matters

meaning   the thread running forever in shadow
Lucille   poet of light   here   now
shifting patterns   light and dark   under-
branches   pussywillow   sun out of this window

and when you were four   bare-foot
on cool kikuyu   under
the plane tree
                    cool comfort   damp grass underfoot
looking up   looking out into the momentary
dark undersides   leaves against the light

before reason's terrible questions
strange   as in asking
God

let alone *symbol of God*
at school in standard three   sweating over *transubstantiation*
weird as *hell*
you can't possibly really think that
your mother   while she is driving   and you are trying to tell
something you only feel like the shadow of shadow shifting

nine   standard three   numbers   now more than
bonds   tables   now this strange   infinity   *eternity*
and now God's body becoming bread becoming body
but even more weird   *Word* –

no words yet even for *weird*   nor for *surreal*
let alone after all these years   Christ!
prototype   archetype   archi-image
your daughter calls pattern after Kierkegaard's call

let me tell you   strangers
in that moment
only sudden sweat on the seat   sticky skin and visceral
constriction

*

Constantly running in shadow
and light
    ripples on the river
rivers of light in the leaves overhead

when you think you almost see it   almost have it   bit by bit
when your words   begin to fit
for the moment
you begin to see you are reaching

intimate strangers
reading your exile your longing   over this screen
how you pattern   your despair   do you ask
who you are reaching who is responding

only you   calls the buff-spotted flufftail
in the lengthening late
only you   summer far gone far away   night

dark underbranch underwater pull
like hidden old logs under our dark-
golden river the Goukamma

words   like floating islands
Ruth Miller's *The Floating Island* Dorothy Wordsworth's
Floating Island surfacing again
lost fragments shall remain/ to fertilise some other ground

words like water lillies
in the long ago dark of the dam named *Amanzimnyama*

fractal surfaces breaking
 open

strangers   over this Zoom   when we are talking
pattern   are we talking
nature   nurture   politics   history
eco-biology psycho-neuro-endocrinology
or in that clunky Edwardian terminology
psycho-physical unity

when the poem knits emotionally   eventually
we stop asking
is it abstract or narrative

*

Look! look up at the leaves
still looking up looking out
the shining against the dark
under branches
a river of ripples
repeated these
patterns like a mother's
here I go again down that old river of dark
she let herself out all night
in that terrible trickle from the temple
pooled in the mattress
the men wanted to burn

years later burnt with everything else
the past past and its lives
up in flames

but look! look what I have here!
on the other side of the earth
pictures of kids in canoes
there they go down that river the day after the memorial
into the shadow where the old man's beard drips
out of the milkwoods into the sun

*

Run   says your beloved son
get your heart pumping
strap on a pair   and get out there

your sister-in-law says   The Church
for years your brothers have been saying
                    for Christ's sake no more wine
o god what can you say

one of the things the tutor says
over the Zoom over the screen
a poet never feels at home

what were you thinking
as you looked out of the kids' empty rooms

listening   practising
firing the under-used neurons
of non-doing as in *negative capability*
inhibiting the need to answer the need
for answers
the urge to do to make it make sense
make something come true

                    the sun   across the valley   come
piecing together
bits and pieces
                    like the ragged old cot cover
                    in the geyser cupboard
never even covered the baby then

where do you think they go
scraps   bits and pieces   scribbled   *leaves*
to a tree   tiny shiny epiphanies
the shadow of the valley
of soul making
not knowing where you're going not banging your head
against your will
like against the brick chimney stack behind your back
where you simply leant in the morning sun
outside your outside room
looking out over patchwork fields

the river   cutting its way
to the mouth

     *

You are
          aware   indirectly
on your back on your bed
in the sun

your ventral vagus nerve wandering off
to your breath and your heart
talking to your daughter on the Whatsapp
listening to the snufflings of her breast-feeding son

tea and cake or whatever it takes in this end of summer sun
allowing yourself
to move more freely as you release those glutes
aware of latissimus dorsi allowing your arms
looseness loosely
you lean to pour the tea
thoughts going their own way
they know
          your mother and daughter
would know or somehow follow   could be with your
daughter
          in this bitter-sweet sun

like those sleepy baboons along the Timbavati
sunning themselves in early morning branches
picking nits from hair   little ones easily underbelly
let them come   grunting
I'm surviving   I am moved

          *

Wake   beyond
the point of no return
after these long covid months and months at last
talking at last listening   walking these old lanes   unravelling
the past

brother in this kitchen
punching himself below the sternum
it feels like barbed wire bundled here

and I am seeing the raised weals of the cane
track across his seven year old back
at least the rules ruled
you don't hit girls

car wheels on the gravel turning circle
yesterday today and tomorrow
flowering its sweetness outside the red brick house
where I lived for a year and a term with a mother's cousin's
wife's surrogate everything
before eight years of boarding school

undoing   simply unstacking the dishwasher
pain shoots from the hip
laying me out on the kitchen floor

*

Rover   the name of the dog in the first reader
like the name of the dinky car and my grandfather's
1956 *model*   the year I was born

years later couldn't get that Rover into reverse
twenty two and all that time   spent   wasted
Smitswinkelsbaai and that tank parked
at the top of the krantz
where   baboons and their barking kept watch

what was I doing down at the cove   undoing
myself in longing fucking telling myself it was love it was fire
like in the sun-lit pattern of pine knots in the planks
   of the cabin
it was fine it was fire
telling myself I could handle it

*

All of that   over

to not have even thought about it
all that hormonal longing
not even in relation to a daughter
or son

to not have thought for so long
about drawing a line
between a life and the future
to not have worried about disease   HIV   AIDS
not condom   nor **IUD**   nor pill

old crone you could say I am now
and what the fuck has happened
to wild abandon   wild will

more like mother-in-law of mysoginist jokes
still cleaning up after everyone
at their after-party bed
little shrivelled bit in the bottom of the used cup
smelling of semen like the warmth

                              of far-off far-gone

milkwoods   seeding   at home

           *

He wanted her so much   my father told us
dear god what could that even mean he would not
let her out of his sight

how come she came
to lie on the bed
like her mother sat on the chair
and literally the same fucking gun

they met after her mother
                         (our grandmother) had done it
he sat outside the lavatory   he told us   waiting for her
the first time they met
he would never let her get away

a party like the party her mother asked her not to go to
the night she went out and off

like so many years later I was up and off
out of there when she started those same laments
and that night   that very same gun

            *

73

More sleep   bit by bit

                even if it brings me men

                aiming guns at my head

                men aiming to crush me between

outrageous pieces

                of machinery   even if it brings

my own old father *Dawie*

collapsed on the floor where I lean to comfort him

as if he were still in need as if he were still as he was

when he was still

his mother's *Ricky*

waking   more waking

to that strange peace of   *stok siel alleen*

sycamore leaves through the skylight window upshoots

of ash

christmas beetles   in my own ears

whispering of leaves   far away   car tyres

        *

I heard about the poet   and his death
               sitting in this sitting-room
listening to the wind   then the still then
Haydn on my phone
                across a sea a continent a continent an age
Haydn reminds me
cave in at the pectorals   at home with grief   where it waits
and you can't do anything   can't even hear

the poor poet's death reminds me
he believed love would somehow save him
from what from whatever he meant he meant he made
his brave boat of love and he lay in that   tender ship his
tendership

wind down now wind gone in   fence across the boundary
through the French windows or are they called doors
the post and rail fence and black branches of ash
and silver sky

poor poet   remind me how to look even here
on the other side
of the earth   see!
              from under the dark
underbranches   across
the long grass   as if from out of a child's picture book
a legend of love
tender   alert   alive   muzzle and antlers
clear as a symbol   dear-heart   heart's companion

like my own grandson   my own   Hart
even across the sea   a continent
my own age   my own   companionship

     *

Eventually I thought I heard
        she did not love life enough and I could not
how could I
        take that terrible freight
helping to kill her
I would not hear
        as I had to   as I can at last
she   as her mother my grandmother
had run out of love –

                    *

Spanish immersion   new pencils and crayons
first lessons   first sweepings across the strings of the violin
and asking for a sticker to take home to her brother
picking tomatoes she has grown   to take to Frankie
piecing her own quilt   patches of pink and *Frozen* –
these are the loves her mother is showing to Cora
her daughter my granddaughter
ways my daughter   Frances   *free woman*

is showing to love –
my core

*

My darlings

        wish I were with you

wish I could come to you

my newest one

        Isaac Thando

thando   mayibuye

"love you to bits and pieces"

    *

5

Listen
hear me hearing the ashes now
over the clock ticking

over the constant measure of time
ash leaves' sussurating timelessness

talking to myself aloud   to the trees   as

as I drive down the drop
from Robertson's field on the corner to the drift at Jan Sak
        purple Outeniquas behind   Groenvlei in front
silver silver-trees
                    listen   listen

in the old silver *kombi*   rattling off to fetch the kids
with windows that won't wind up
like a world war one fighter pilot
coat hood over ears against the cold open air
just before the level crossing
                    just after their granny shoots herself –

                *

Remind me
what is required of me
can I do no more
than notice
the voice   *too much me too much ego   I*

can it be the sky
is as true today as under
African sun   African sky

somewhere someone I can hear saying
after the pie-cart-man in the village
nice day   perfect

face cold to the north
back to the sun
someone calling in the dry leaves still
I can't tell who

half-hearing the horses
grinding the grass   snorting out seeds
waiting again at the empty bucket
at the corner of the field
where the pipe has come adrift
 buzzards above crying
            like African wild cats into the blue

now the callers have come out
to sun themselves and now they're shouting
on the fence

two wrens   at each other   and now   two little tits
at it again   whatever it is   as if it were
all necessary what they are doing today

there they go   they know how to do it
get out of their own way out of this
                    emptiness
ordinary love to be heard   *I write what I like*

          *

And now to make new spaces
                              sacred now
thinking out to the ordinary old
ancient almost
dry river beds with ancient
jakalsbessie   marula   tamboti
down the dry watercourse
in the dark shining
eyes just before dawn in the car lights along the dips
in the track morning lion eyes burning into
the inner retina

and at home   the southern cross   hanging
above the dune and the southernmost coast

through the valley of the shadow
brown black river like the wandering vagus
nerve to the heart

            *

Despite that insane intensity   long ago

> imprisoned with grief for a suicide mother

> breaking out feral with falling for a Russian writer
> with the safety of a Swiss summer and its deep
> maternal green

> asked for it   was given it
> as if I didn't deserve it

despite the vilifying admonishment
momentary gold
month to month at home
molten in the river   the rising moon

now again in the sycamore leaves
here in the north
before the season's end

as in leaning over at the side of the road
> through the little karoo   giving
> taking that kiss   37 years ago
> unable to resist
burnished poplar spines'
upthrust into the blue

despite this unshelteredness   the two of us

> *no job   no pension*

nearly depleted money like fairy-tale pot-of-gold
like the rich of the earth
here we are still
a cottage   kind landlord   faithful four-footed friend
cacophonous news and
music of the universe

through the two little earbuds I gave him
little stalks at his ears like a tender insect
at home

                    *

Even in a new country   even along unknown ancient lanes
under foreign trees foreign birdsong along foreign
public footpaths worn with centuries of intimate foot-fall

seven hundreds of years gone they came up this hill
for the woad for their wool   *Waddon* it's called still
and *Barton* for the house that was the homestead
along the ridge the wall
and behind the wall the lord
straight out of my own ruled
hard-covered brown-paper-covered
middle-ages standard-three history book

a continent   an age
eleven official languages and their histories   away

the gate at the dam in the dip
the sign as if from my own childhood
slow   ducks   crossing

while you're walking thinking of something else entirely
they come up on you   running feet
the ways worn with the footsteps of the dead
and now   like lost children come again running

                    *

Invisible voices
two in the morning   cold   like owls   like lovers
like those who never really wanted me
all through this northern winter
                    as I thought of returning
dreaming myself
                    as my great-aunt Katinkie

burning out the end of a life   alone
at the edge of the rocks
at the edge of unswimmable southern sea

        *

www.ingramcontent.com/pod-product-compliance
Lightning Source LLC
Chambersburg PA
CBHW070334090426
42733CB00012B/2480